SUMMARY OF NUMBERS THAT PROPHESY

Hearing God Through Historic Headlines and Numbers That Preach

TROY A. BREWER

D DESTINY IMAGE

Copyright 2024–Destiny Image

All rights reserved. This book is protected by the copyright laws of the United States of America. This book may not be copied or reprinted for commercial gain or profit. The use of short quotations or occasional page copying for personal or group study is permitted and encouraged. Permission will be granted upon request. Unless otherwise indicated, all scripture quotations are taken from the *King James Version* of the Bible. Used by permission. All rights reserved.

All emphasis within Scripture quotations is the author's own. Please note that Destiny Image's publishing style capitalizes certain pronouns in Scripture that refer to the Father, Son, and Holy Spirit, and may differ from some publishers' styles. Take note that the name satan and related names are not capitalized. We choose not to acknowledge him, even to the point of violating grammatical rules.

Destiny Image P.O. Box 310, Shippensburg, PA 17257-0310

This book and all other Destiny Image's books are available at Christian bookstores and distributors worldwide.

For Worldwide Distribution.

Reach us on the Internet: www.destinyimage.com.

ISBN 13 TP: 9780768481723

ISBN 13 eBook: 9780768483031

CONTENTS

Introduction	v
1. Prophetic Historic Event 1: President Lincoln and the Civil War	1
2. Prophetic Historic Event 2: The RMS Titanic	5
3. Prophetic Historic Event 3: "Man" on the Moon	9
4. Prophetic Historic Event 4: The Space Shuttle Columbia	13
5. Prophetic Historic Event 5: Princess Diana and Mother Teresa	17
6. Prophetic Historic Event 6: 9/11 Terrorist Attacks on the United States of America	21
7. The Hype of Type	25
8. Last Words	29
About the Publisher	33

INTRODUCTION

Welcome to the enlightening world of "Numbers That Prophesy," a guide that explores the profound spiritual significance behind numbers as referenced in the Bible. This summary aims to provide a concise understanding of how numbers are not just arbitrary figures but carry divine meanings that have been used by God to communicate His purposes throughout biblical history.

In this text, each number—from one to seventy and beyond—has been meticulously analyzed to uncover its scriptural symbolism and prophetic significance. From creation to revelation, numbers are shown to be a fundamental element through which God expresses His order, precision, and even mysteries. For instance, the number seven signifies completeness and perfection, often associated with God's creation and rest, while twelve represents divine government and authority, as seen in the twelve tribes of Israel and the twelve apostles.

INTRODUCTION

This summary serves as a gateway for believers and scholars alike to deepen their understanding of scriptural narratives and to perceive the world around them through a biblically enriched perspective. By delving into the biblical numerology presented in "Numbers That Prophesy," readers are invited to explore how these numbers can influence their interpretation of events, enhance their spiritual walk, and foster a greater appreciation for the intricacies of God's design.

Whether you are a seasoned theologian, a new student of the Bible, or someone curious about the intersection of faith and numerology, this summary offers valuable insights into how numbers manifest in scripture and in our everyday lives. It encourages readers to reflect on the omnipresence of divine orchestration, urging a contemplative approach to both historical and present-day phenomena as guided by the profound truths hidden within sacred numbers.

As we embark on this journey through the numerical landscape of the Bible, let us open our hearts and minds to the deeper revelations that await. Embrace the opportunity to see the world through a lens of divine order and prophetic insight, and let the numbers lead you closer to understanding the heart and mind of God.

CHAPTER 1

PROPHETIC HISTORIC EVENT 1: PRESIDENT LINCOLN AND THE CIVIL WAR

Bible Verse

"For it is God's will that by doing good you should silence the ignorant talk of foolish people." - 1 Peter 2:15 (NIV)

Introduction

This chapter delves into the prophetic significance of President Abraham Lincoln's life and assassination, viewing historical events through a spiritual lens to uncover deeper meanings. It highlights Lincoln's prophetic dream just days before his death, connecting it with the broader impact of his leadership and the Civil War on America's destiny.

Word of Wisdom

"It is the glory of God to conceal a matter, but the glory of kings is to search out a matter." (Proverbs 25:2 NKJV)

Main Theme

The chapter explores the idea that significant historical events, specifically the assassination of President Lincoln and the outcomes of the Civil War, carry prophetic messages that reflect God's intervention in human affairs.

Key Points

- Abraham Lincoln had a prophetic dream about his assassination, which he shared with friends just days before it occurred.
- Lincoln's leadership during the Civil War, particularly his efforts towards ending slavery, can be viewed as divinely inspired.
- The timing of Lincoln's death coincides with significant religious observances, suggesting a deeper spiritual significance.
- Numerological analysis of dates and names related to Lincoln reveals potential prophetic insights.
- Lincoln's death marks not just the end of his life but a profound transformative moment for the entire nation.
- The impact of the Civil War and Lincoln's policies had lasting effects on the spiritual and social fabric of the United States.

Key Themes

- **Prophetic Dreams and Premonitions:** Abraham Lincoln's unsettling dream of his own death just days before it happened

serves as a profound reflection of his subconscious awareness of the nation's turmoil and possibly, divine insights into his fate.
- **Divine Timing and Symbolism:** The assassination occurring around Passover and Good Friday underlines a biblical parallel, portraying Lincoln as a Christ-like figure whose death was intertwined with themes of sacrifice and redemption.
- **The Role of Numerology in Prophecy:** Names, dates, and numbers associated with Lincoln and the Civil War are explored for their hidden meanings, suggesting that God communicates through the details of history.
- **Impact of Lincoln's Leadership:** Lincoln's policies, particularly the Emancipation Proclamation and the push for the 13th Amendment, are seen as fulfillment of divine justice, positioning him as a pivotal figure in the spiritual battle against slavery.
- **Historical Impact of the Civil War:** The Civil War is contextualized not just as a political conflict but as a spiritual crucible for the nation, with lasting repercussions on America's moral and spiritual direction.
- **Prophetic Interpretation of Events:** This theme encourages readers to view historical events through a prophetic lens, suggesting that understanding the spiritual implications behind them can offer guidance and wisdom for contemporary issues.

Conclusion

The assassination of President Lincoln and the Civil War are portrayed not merely as historical events but as moments laden with divine significance. Through prophetic interpretation, these events reveal God's active presence in shaping the nation's destiny. This perspective invites readers to reflect on how divine patterns and purposes might be discernable in modern times, urging a deeper consideration of historical and current events in the light of God's Word.

CHAPTER 2

PROPHETIC HISTORIC EVENT 2: THE RMS TITANIC

Bible Verse
"But by the mouth of two or three witnesses every word shall be established." - 2 Corinthians 13:1 (NKJV)

Introduction

This chapter examines the prophetic significance of the Titanic disaster, drawing parallels with historical events and prophetic messages. It highlights the premonitions and literary predictions that eerily foretold the fate of the Titanic, tying these elements to broader spiritual themes and interpretations.

Word of Wisdom

"God does not cause tragedies, but He employs them to speak to each generation." Troy Brewer

Main Theme

The sinking of the Titanic serves as a profound prophetic symbol, representing the dangers of human pride and the necessity of heeding divine warnings.

Key Points

- The Titanic disaster occurred on the same dates as Abraham Lincoln's assassination, linking these events prophetically.
- W.T. Stead, a passenger on the Titanic, had previously written about a similar disaster in fiction, highlighting the concept of prophetic foreshadowing.
- The lack of lifeboats on the Titanic, which Stead had warned about in his writings, was a critical factor in the high casualty rate.
- Various ships warned the Titanic of ice, but these warnings were ignored, symbolizing spiritual and physical recklessness.
- The Titanic represented the pinnacle of human achievement and pride, yet it met with a catastrophic end.
- Both literary and personal premonitions about the Titanic's fate emphasize a prophetic message of caution and reflection.

Key Themes

- **Prophetic Premonitions and Historical Parallels:** The striking coincidences between the dates of the Titanic disaster and Lincoln's assassination suggest a deeper prophetic connection, inviting reflection on the potential meanings behind significant historical dates.
- **Warnings Ignored:** The Titanic received multiple warnings about icebergs from nearby ships, yet these were disregarded due to distractions and overconfidence. This theme underscores the spiritual lesson of listening to and heeding warnings, both divine and earthly.
- **Human Pride and Divine Intervention:** The Titanic is portrayed as a symbol of human arrogance, challenging the divine with its presumed unsinkability. The disaster serves as a stark reminder of the limits of human endeavor and the ultimate authority of God.
- **The Role of Media and Prophetic Voices:** W.T. Stead's life and work, including his accurate fictional prediction of a maritime disaster, highlight the role of media figures in shaping public perception and potentially echoing prophetic truths.
- **Spiritual Reflection and Response:** The chapter encourages a spiritual interpretation of historical events, urging readers to consider how God might be speaking through tragedies and to respond

by aligning more closely with divine will and wisdom.

Conclusion

The Titanic's tragic end is more than a historical event; it is a prophetic narrative about the consequences of ignoring divine warnings and the perils of human pride. This chapter calls for a contemplative approach to history, recognizing God's voice in the midst of human achievements and failures, and encourages a humble and attentive posture towards the lessons that history and prophecy impart.

CHAPTER 3

PROPHETIC HISTORIC EVENT 3: "MAN" ON THE MOON

Bible Verse

"For God has not given us a spirit of fear, but of power and of love and of a sound mind." (2 Timothy 1:7 NKJV)

Introduction

This chapter delves into the prophetic significance of the Apollo 11 moon landing, interpreting the events and outcomes as divine messages of overcoming fear, sin, and death. The narrative connects historical facts with biblical numerology to draw profound spiritual lessons from this monumental human achievement.

Word of Wisdom

"God will use whatever He wants to display His glory. Heavens and stars. History and nations. People and problems." – Max Lucado

Main Theme

The chapter explores the Apollo 11 moon mission through a prophetic lens, suggesting that the event was not merely a technological triumph but also a spiritual signpost pointing towards human capability, divine providence, and the overcoming of earthly and spiritual challenges.

Key Points

- Neil Armstrong's moon landing speech and the unplanned events during Apollo 11's landing are seen as prophetic and filled with spiritual significance.
- The number six and its occurrences throughout the mission are discussed in depth, relating to man's creation and inherent nature.
- The historic moon landing is linked to various biblical scriptures and the prophetic implications of the numbers involved.
- The roles of Armstrong, Aldrin, and Collins are prophetically analyzed with their names and mission details providing spiritual metaphors.
- The moon dust brought back by Apollo 11 raises both scientific and spiritual discussions about man's origin and destiny.
- The overall impact of Apollo 11 is viewed as a testament to human courage and divine guidance, setting a precedent for future explorations and spiritual revelations.

SUMMARY OF NUMBERS THAT PROPHESY

Key Themes

- **Prophetic Names and Numbers:** The names of the Apollo 11 crew members and the mission's numerical details are interpreted to reveal divine messages, with Armstrong's missing "a" in his famous quote considered a significant prophetic slip, linking directly to Romans in the Bible.
- **Spiritual Significance of Moon Dust:** The moon dust, feared to be potentially hazardous, symbolizes the biblical 'dust of the earth' from which man was created, suggesting a divine connection between creation, exploration, and revelation.
- **Technological Triumph and Divine Approval:** The successful landing, despite numerous challenges, is portrayed as a manifestation of God's grace, with the technological achievements of the mission seen as being underpinned by divine support.
- **Legacy and Prophetic Interpretation:** The legacy of the Apollo 11 mission is framed within a prophetic narrative, suggesting that the historical event was preordained and holds ongoing spiritual significance for mankind.
- **The Role of Fear and Overcoming:** The chapter emphasizes the theme of overcoming fear through faith, aligning the astronauts' experiences with biblical admonitions about fear, power, love, and sound mind.

- **Interconnectedness of Science and Spirituality:** The exploration of space is presented not just as a scientific endeavor but as a spiritual journey, highlighting the interconnectedness of human achievements and divine truths.

Conclusion

This analysis of the Apollo 11 moon landing as a prophetic historic event invites readers to view scientific achievements through a spiritual lens, encouraging a deeper understanding of how divine messages can manifest in modern human endeavors. The chapter reinforces the belief that God's presence is evident in the vastness of space and in the minutiae of numbers and names, calling on mankind to recognize and respond to these divine signals with faith and courage.

CHAPTER 4

PROPHETIC HISTORIC EVENT 4: THE SPACE SHUTTLE COLUMBIA

Bible Verse

"Remember therefore from where you have fallen; repent and do the first works, or else I will come to you quickly and remove your lampstand from its place—unless you repent." (Revelation 2:5 NKJV)

Introduction

This chapter interprets the tragic loss of the Space Shuttle Columbia and its crew as a divine message to America, urging a return to foundational spiritual commitments. It sees the disaster as a parable about vulnerability, judgment, and the necessity of maintaining a first love for God amidst technological and national achievements.

Word of Wisdom

"In Him (God), history and prophecy

are one and the same." —Aiden Wilson Tozer

Main Theme

The chapter argues that the Columbia disaster serves as a prophetic warning to America, emphasizing the need for spiritual vigilance and repentance. It explores the event through the lens of biblical numerology and symbolism, suggesting that even great achievements must be grounded in spiritual truth and humility.

Key Points

• The Space Shuttle Columbia disaster is viewed as a prophetic symbol of America's need to return to its spiritual foundations.

• The event is paralleled with biblical stories where disaster befalls the good and the godly, challenging assumptions about divine protection.

• Key figures and aspects of the mission are interpreted as symbolic of broader spiritual messages.

• The timing and details of the disaster are linked to specific biblical numerologies, emphasizing judgment and the need for repentance.

• The chapter calls for a reassessment of national priorities, aligning them more closely with divine commands and guidance.

SUMMARY OF NUMBERS THAT PROPHESY

Key Themes

- **Prophetic Symbolism of Crew and Mission:** Each member of the Columbia crew is seen not just as an individual but as a symbol within a larger divine message, with their collective tragedy pointing to America's spiritual state and the need for a national reassessment of priorities.
- **Biblical Numerology and Interpretation:** The dates, times, and numerical details of the Columbia disaster are analyzed in relation to biblical scripture, suggesting that these elements prophesy divine judgment and a call to repentance, underscoring the urgency of returning to foundational spiritual values.
- **Implications of Technological Advancements:** While technological advancements symbolize human progress, the chapter warns that these should not lead to hubris or a departure from spiritual devotion, as exemplified by the Columbia disaster.
- **National and Spiritual Identity:** Columbia, as a symbol for America, brings into focus the theme of national identity intertwined with spiritual destiny, urging a reflection on how America's historical missions align with biblical principles.
- **Call to Action and Reflection:** The disaster serves as a wake-up call for introspection and change, emphasizing that true security and success are found not in technological might but in spiritual alignment and obedience to God.

Conclusion

The Space Shuttle Columbia disaster is portrayed not just as a national tragedy but as a divine signal calling for a return to spiritual priorities. The chapter serves as a reminder of the impermanence of human achievements and the eternal significance of spiritual fidelity, urging America to heed the lessons of history and scripture to avert future spiritual and physical calamities.

CHAPTER 5

PROPHETIC HISTORIC EVENT 5: PRINCESS DIANA AND MOTHER TERESA

Bible Verse

"Anyone with ears to hear should listen and understand!" (Matthew 11:15 NLT)

Introduction

This chapter explores the prophetic symbolism in the near-simultaneous deaths of Princess Diana and Mother Teresa. Both women, through their lives and deaths, represent contrasting visions of worldly allure versus spiritual devotion, serving as potent symbols for deeper biblical truths about grace, beauty, and the human condition.

Word of Wisdom

"The vague and tenuous hope that God is too kind to punish the ungodly has become a deadly opiate for the consciences of millions." —A. W. Tozer

Main Theme

The contrasting deaths of Princess Diana and Mother Teresa symbolize the dichotomy between secular glamour and selfless service, posing a stark reminder of the spiritual lessons and biblical prophecies reflected in their lives and legacies.

Key Points

• Princess Diana's tragic death symbolizes the dangers of worldly pursuits and the fleeting nature of secular adoration.

• Mother Teresa's peaceful passing represents a life of grace and selfless service, marked by the favor of God.

• The number 5 in Mother Teresa's life highlights divine grace, while the numbers associated with Diana's death (666, 13) symbolize complete flesh and rebellion.

• Both women's deaths serve as prophetic messages to the church, reflecting the consequences of spiritual choices.

• Diana and Mother Teresa are depicted as symbolic figures in a broader divine narrative, each teaching lessons about grace, sacrifice, and the vanity of earthly pleasures.

Key Themes

- **Symbolism of Their Lives and Deaths:** Princess Diana and Mother Teresa embody two different aspects of human existence and spiritual symbolism. Diana's life and sudden, tragic death reflect the perils of living a life centered on worldly values, while Mother Teresa's peaceful demise underscores a life lived in alignment with divine grace and service.

- **Prophetic Interpretations and Biblical Numerology:** The prophetic significance of the numbers associated with their lives and deaths (like 5, 666, and 13) serves to underline the spiritual lessons their stories convey. These numbers reveal deeper insights into God's grace, human rebellion, and the spiritual warfare waged in the lives of believers and non-believers alike.
- **Contrasting Public Reactions and Legacies:** The world's intense focus on Diana, contrasted with the quieter recognition of Mother Teresa's death, illustrates the different values celebrated by society versus those honored by God. This disparity highlights the biblical principle that what is esteemed by humans is often detestable in God's sight.
- **Lessons for the Church:** The chapter uses the lives of these two women to critique and instruct the church on proper Christian values, emphasizing the importance of true discipleship and the dangers of conforming to worldly patterns.
- **Call to Spiritual Vigilance and Repentance:** Their stories serve as a call to the church to maintain vigilance in its spiritual commitments and to repent where necessary. The narrative encourages

a reevaluation of priorities, urging a return to the first love of Christ to avoid spiritual decay and ensure eternal rewards.

Conclusion

Princess Diana and Mother Teresa's lives and deaths provide profound lessons on the spiritual dichotomy between secular allure and godly humility. This chapter urges believers to discern and embrace the lessons of their legacies, advocating for a life of service over one of self-centered pursuits, and calls for a return to the fundamental values of love and service as taught by Christ.

CHAPTER 6

PROPHETIC HISTORIC EVENT 6: 9/11 TERRORIST ATTACKS ON THE UNITED STATES OF AMERICA

Bible Verse

"Thus I establish My covenant with you: Never again shall all flesh be cut off by the waters of the flood; never again shall there be a flood to destroy the earth." (Genesis 9:11 NKJV)

Introduction

This chapter delves into the prophetic significance of the 9/11 terrorist attacks, a day of immense tragedy that reshaped America and sparked a national revival. It explores how God prepared the author with visions and messages that foreshadowed the event and its aftermath, emphasizing the importance of understanding God's messages conveyed through numbers and events.

Word of Wisdom

"You start seeing a pattern, or you

start seeing some kind of a prophetic pattern, so you know that it's the Lord; but just because God is speaking and you know it's Him doesn't mean you understand it." Troy Brewer

Main Theme

The 9/11 attacks are portrayed not just as a national tragedy but as a divine message about judgment and disorder, pointing towards a necessary return to God amidst chaos.

Key Points

• The author was spiritually prepared for 9/11 with prophetic messages two years prior to the event.

• 9/11 sparked a significant national revival where many turned to God.

• The numbers 9 and 11 symbolize judgment and disorder, providing a deeper spiritual message about the events.

• Immediate aftermath included a symbolic national mourning, represented by people covered in ashes.

• The attacks are a call to understand God's judgment and the need for repentance and return to divine order.

SUMMARY OF NUMBERS THAT PROPHESY

Key Themes

- **Prophetic Preparation and Immediate Impact:** The author emphasizes that he was divinely prepared for the 9/11 attacks, which allowed him to offer timely spiritual guidance when it was most needed. The immediate impact of the attacks catalyzed a national revival, with many Americans turning to faith amidst the chaos.
- **Symbolic Interpretation of Numbers:** In the text, numbers play a significant role, with 9 symbolizing judgment and 11 indicating disorder. These numbers are used to interpret the events of 9/11 as a divine message, urging a deeper contemplation of spiritual alignment and national identity.
- **National Mourning and Spiritual Reflection:** The imagery of Americans covered in ashes is used to symbolize national mourning. This motif is tied to biblical practices of mourning and repentance, reinforcing the theme of turning to God in times of national crisis.
- **Revival and the Role of the Church:** Post-9/11, there was a marked increase in religious fervor across the United States. The author suggests that this was a fulfillment of a prophetic vision indicating a spiritual awakening or revival, highlighting the church's pivotal role during crises.
- **Future Implications and Call to Action:** The chapter concludes with a call

to heed the lessons of 9/11, suggesting that understanding and responding to divine messages can prevent future calamities and lead to spiritual renewal.

Conclusion

The 9/11 terrorist attacks serve as a profound reminder of the need for spiritual vigilance and the importance of deciphering God's messages in our lives. This tragic day is portrayed not only as a moment of loss but as a catalyst for national reflection, spiritual awakening, and a deeper understanding of divine judgment and order. The author urges a continued pursuit of this understanding to foster a national environment guided by divine principles.

CHAPTER 7

THE HYPE OF TYPE

Bible Verse

"But the Helper, the Holy Spirit, whom the Father will send in My name, He will teach you all things and bring to your remembrance all that I have said to you." (John 14:26 NKJV)

Introduction

This chapter explores the various ways God communicates with His people through types, shadows, symbols, numbers, and secrets. It emphasizes the importance of understanding and being attentive to these divine communications to deepen one's spiritual walk and alignment with God's will.

Word of Wisdom

"God is speaking to you right now, and it is a word that changes everything."
Troy Brewer

Main Theme

The main theme focuses on the significance of typology in understanding divine messages and the essential role of the Holy Spirit in revealing and interpreting God's communications through various symbolic means.

Key Points

• God uses typology to speak through symbols, numbers, and historical patterns.

• Recognizing and understanding these types speaks to our relationship and intimacy with God.

• The Holy Spirit plays a crucial role in teaching and reminding believers of God's words.

• Historical and biblical events often carry prophetic significance that can be relevant today.

• Each believer has the potential to hear and interpret God's messages if they are spiritually attuned.

Key Themes

- **Prophetic Understanding of Historical Events:** The chapter discusses how significant historical dates like the 9th of Av have held recurring patterns of tragedy due to disobedience, highlighting the need for awareness and repentance.
- **The Role of the Holy Spirit in Revelation:** It emphasizes the role of the

Holy Spirit as a teacher who brings clarity to the hidden messages in God's word, helping believers recall and understand the divine truths relevant to their lives.
- **The Impact of Divine Communication:** Understanding God's messages through types and shadows not only enriches personal faith but also prepares believers to respond appropriately to His will, enhancing their spiritual journey and relationship with God.
- **Integration of Prophetic Insights in Daily Life:** The chapter encourages believers to incorporate their understanding of God's messages into everyday life, ensuring that their actions and decisions align with divine insights.
- **The Importance of Spiritual Sensitivity:** It stresses the importance of developing a sensitivity to the spiritual dimensions of God's communication, allowing believers to discern and act upon His guidance more effectively.

Conclusion

The exploration of typology as a means of divine communication underscores the richness of God's interactions with His people. By engaging with and understanding the symbols, types, and shadows presented in the Scriptures and everyday life, believers can deepen their relationship with God, becoming more attuned to His voice and His workings in the world. This chapter calls for a heartfelt pursuit of the knowledge and wisdom that

comes from recognizing and interpreting the ways
God speaks to us today.

CHAPTER 8

LAST WORDS

Romans 10:17 (NKJV) "So then faith comes by hearing, and hearing by the word of God."

Introduction

This chapter explores the continuous and multifaceted ways God communicates with humanity, emphasizing the importance of recognizing His voice, especially in challenging times. It serves as a guide to understanding the prophetic nature of God's communication, connecting past events with the present and future through a spiritual lens.

Word of Wisdom

"Just because something terrible happens doesn't mean that God's amazing heart cannot be heard within it." – Troy Brewer

Main Theme

The main theme of "Last Words" is the prophetic understanding of God's communications. It stresses that prophecy is not merely about foretelling future events but about deeply knowing God's heart and recognizing His voice in every situation.

Key Points

• God's voice has historically been a guiding force, and it remains just as relevant today.

• Recognizing God's communication requires a focus on Jesus and an understanding of God's nature.

• Prophetic insights offer a means to connect with God's heart, especially during crises.

• God speaks through various events and symbols, which are reflections of His will and teachings.

• Engaging with the prophetic can deepen one's faith and understanding of divine intentions.

• Sharing these insights can foster spiritual discussions and growth among friends and family.

Key Themes

- **Historical Continuity of God's Voice:** God has consistently communicated with humanity throughout history, showing that His guidance is timeless and crucial for spiritual growth and understanding.

- **Prophetic Nature of God's Communications:** More than predicting future events, prophecy involves understanding God's heart and intentions, turning seemingly random or tragic events into moments of divine revelation.
- **Engagement with the Prophetic:** Actively engaging with the prophetic aspect of faith can transform personal and communal understanding of events, encouraging a deeper spiritual dialogue within one's community.
- **Understanding Through Symbols:** God often speaks through symbols and events, each carrying profound spiritual significance that, when interpreted correctly, can reveal His desires and guidance for His people.
- **Practical Application of Prophetic Insights:** By recognizing and discussing prophetic insights in everyday life, believers can use these moments to strengthen their faith and share God's word with others, making the prophetic a practical part of daily life.

Conclusion

"Last Words" encourages believers to continually seek and recognize God's voice across all aspects of life. By understanding that God communicates not just through the scriptures but through every unfolding event and symbol around us, believers can maintain hope and deepen their faith, seeing the divine hand at work in all circumstances. This recognition fosters a more profound connection

with God, enriching one's spiritual journey and
enhancing the communal faith experience.

▫ DESTINY IMAGE

Destiny Image is a prophetic Christian publisher dedicated to empowering believers through Spirit-led messages. Our mission is to equip and inspire individuals to fulfill their God-given destinies by providing transformative resources that resonate with the Charismatic and Pentecostal faith.

We specialize in books, blogs, and back cover copies that reflect prophetic insights, dynamic teachings, and testimonies of faith. Our commitment to fostering spiritual growth and kingdom impact makes Destiny Image a beacon for those seeking to deepen their relationship with God and embrace their calling in the power of the Holy Spirit.

www.ingramcontent.com/pod-product-compliance
Lightning Source LLC
LaVergne TN
LVHW052256070426
835507LV00035B/3085